Your Special Gift
Carol McCormick

Scripture quotations are from The Holy Bible, New International
Version (NIV), Copyright © 1973, 1978, 1984 by the International
Bible Society. Used by permission of Zondervan Publishing House.

Printed in the United States of America

A NOTE TO PARENTS

Having "the talk" with a child about sex can sometimes be an awkward experience for both parties. After squirming in my seat while watching family television shows deal with the subjects of rape and prostitution (while in the company of my nine and eleven-year old daughters), I faced my fears and dealt with this touchy subject in a simple, straightforward and sensitive way.

I didn't want to wait until their hormones kicked in or want them to grow up with misconceptions concerning sex, and I didn't want to be caught off guard when they had questions. I remember one such tense moment from my own childhood: Our family sat watching a police story on television when my younger sister innocently inquired, "What's rape?" An eerie silence came over the room as all eyes immediately turned to Mom. She mumbled an inaudible reply, and we finished watching the show no wiser.

In order to deter any mis-"conceptions," I wanted my children to be informed about the facts of life. Yet, without being too sexually explicit in the process, because some of the facts weren't good such as rape, prostitution, pornography and AIDS.

As a result, I told them what I have written here in an analogy of sex, comparing their bodies to precious gifts, and opening their gifts to having sex.

I wrapped a box in white paper and decorated it with gold stars. Then, I topped it with a bow and this is how I presented it . . .

To my daughters Amy and Tracy

I love Christmas, don't you? It's great! We decorate the tree and hang bright lights, frost cookies and eat candy canes, but the most exciting part of all is the presents!

We can hardly wait until Christmas morning so we can dive under the tree and open our gifts.

Sometimes we feel like we'll go crazy just waiting!

Did you know that your body is a beautiful, precious gift? And waiting until marriage to have sex is like waiting until Christmas to open the gift?

You've heard the word – sex – probably from television or from older kids at school, but do you know what it means?

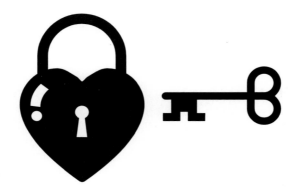

There are lots of names for sex: sleeping together, making love, intercourse, doing it, and many other words that are sometimes used as swear words. But no matter which of these words are used, they all mean the same thing: a man and a woman joining their bodies in an act that most people refer to as having sex.

A man's body part works like a key and a woman's body part works like a lock, and as they fit together they open this wonderful gift.

And they will become one flesh

Genesis 2:24

God intended that this gift be opened by a man and a woman after they get married. In fact, another name for marriage is wedlock.

When a husband and wife open their gifts, they also open their hearts. This union locks them together in a special way like no other relationship does.

The lock in wedlock is for the man and woman's benefit, because sex outside of marriage is less than God's best for their lives.

A man will leave his father and
mother and be united to his wife

Genesis 2:24

What if Christmas morning came and your gift had been opened months before? It wouldn't be a very special day and there wouldn't be a surprise to look forward to.

Or what if someone brought you his or her gift and it had been opened before? You could still love it as much, but it would have been nice to share in the newness together.

Love is kind
1 Corinthians 13:4

Sometimes girls and boys don't mean to open their gifts, but curiosity gets the best of them. They wonder what's in this gift that they've heard so much about. They begin fooling with the tape and feeling through the wrapper (then under the wrapper) and untying the bow, making it a little easier each time to move onto the next step.

This becomes so exciting to them, that before they realize it, they have opened their gifts when they didn't mean to, and it's too late to take back the consequences.

A baby may be growing inside of the girl, or if one of them has a disease, it may be growing inside both of them now.

Love is patient
1 Corinthians 13:4

Some boys see gift opening as a challenge, almost like a game. A boy like this will trick a girl into believing that he cares about her, when all he really cares about is opening her gift. He may say nice things about a girl's gift like it's the most beautiful one he's ever seen, or that she has an especially beautiful part to her gift (like her eyes or smile).

Don't be fooled. If a boy is overly interested in a girl's package, these are usually "lines" to get her to open her gift.

Love is not self-seeking
1 Corinthians 13:5

Some girls open their gifts because they think it will make them more popular, and it may, but for all the wrong reasons. When this happens, the girls are not popular for who they are, but for what they give.

These girls are usually called names that aren't nice and once they are labeled with a bad name, it will usually stick with them for many years.

Girls are valuable just as they are. They don't need to open their gifts to be popular.

Locks protect things that have value

When a girl is paid money for opening her gift, she is called a prostitute or a hooker. And when someone allows his or her unwrapped gift to be photographed for magazines, films or the Internet, this is usually called pornography.

Prostitution and pornography are like taking gifts and placing them in the mud. When people get involved in these things, they not only get mud on their hands, they get mud on their hearts.

Blessed are the pure in heart,
for they will see God

Matthew 5:8

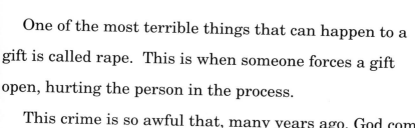

One of the most terrible things that can happen to a gift is called rape. This is when someone forces a gift open, hurting the person in the process.

This crime is so awful that, many years ago, God commanded that the person, who is called a rapist, be killed.

Today the person may go to prison.

Love always protects

1 Corinthians 13:7

You've probably heard the word contagious in reference to someone who has a cold. This means that it's catchy.

There is another very important reason to wait until marriage before you open your gift and that is to prevent the spread of the deadly disease AIDS.

Some of the most common ways that this disease is spread is by sharing a needle of an infected person (using drugs), being born with it because your mother has it, or having sex with an infected person.

The scary thing is that you can't tell by looking at a person if he or she has it or not! That person may not even know if he or she has it himself or herself until it's too late.

God put the lock in wedlock
to keep us safe

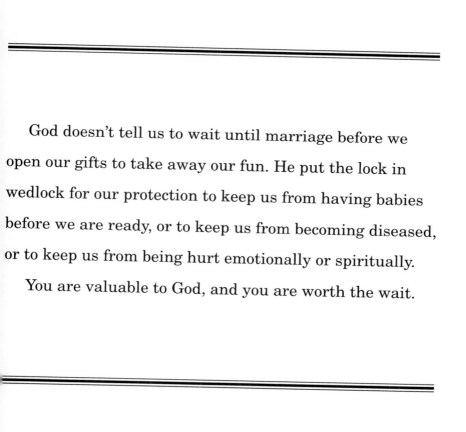

God doesn't tell us to wait until marriage before we open our gifts to take away our fun. He put the lock in wedlock for our protection to keep us from having babies before we are ready, or to keep us from becoming diseased, or to keep us from being hurt emotionally or spiritually.

You are valuable to God, and you are worth the wait.

Love is patient, love is kind.
It does not envy, it does not boast,
it is not proud. It is not rude, it is
not self-seeking, it is not easily
angered, it keeps no record of
wrongs. Love does not delight in
evil but rejoices with the truth. It
always protects, always trusts,
always hopes, always perseveres.
Love never fails.

1 Corinthians 13:4-8a

One final thing . . .

Sometimes a grown-up will get really mixed up about sex and try to open a boy or a girl's gift; the person could even be a relative. When this happens, the older person may think that it's okay to touch or open a boy or girl's gift.

It's not! No one is allowed to touch you in any way that makes you feel uncomfortable, or open your gift in any way just because they are a grown-up friend or relative. If this is happening to you, you are allowed to say, "No!"

It is very important that you tell someone if this has happened to you. Go to your mother, your aunt, your grandmother, or a teacher and tell them what is going on. If this is too hard for you to talk about, go to the person who gave you this book and show him or her, this page. He or she will understand and help you make it stop.

ABOUT THE AUTHOR

Carol McCormick lives in Dunkirk, New York, with her husband, John, and their two daughters, Amy and Tracy. She has been a speaker for the Women's Christian Club, an affiliation of Stonecroft Ministries International.